Josiah Quincy, American Peace Society

The Coming Peace

Josiah Quincy, American Peace Society

The Coming Peace

ISBN/EAN: 9783337217730

Printed in Europe, USA, Canada, Australia, Japan

Cover: Foto ©Suzi / pixelio.de

More available books at **www.hansebooks.com**

THE COMING PEACE.

ORATION

DELIVERED BEFORE THE

CITY COUNCIL AND CITIZENS OF BOSTON,

ON THE

ONE HUNDRED AND FIFTEENTH ANNIVERSARY OF
THE DECLARATION OF INDEPENDENCE,

JULY 4, 1891,

BY

JOSIAH QUINCY.

AMERICAN PEACE SOCIETY,
No. 1 SOMERSET STREET.
1891.

THE COMING PEACE.

ORATION

DELIVERED BEFORE THE

CITY COUNCIL AND CITIZENS OF BOSTON,

ON THE

ONE HUNDRED AND FIFTEENTH ANNIVERSARY OF
THE DECLARATION OF INDEPENDENCE,

JULY 4, 1891,

BY

JOSIAH QUINCY.

AMERICAN PEACE SOCIETY,
No. 1 Somerset Street.
1891.

PRESS OF ROCKWELL & CHURCHILL
BOSTON

1 SOMERSET ST., BOSTON, July 13, 1891.

JOSIAH QUINCY, ESQ. : —

DEAR SIR, — Allow me to hand you a copy of Resolutions unanimously adopted by the Executive Committee of the American Peace Society, July 13, 1891 : —

"*Resolved*, That the thanks of the American Peace Society are hereby extended to Josiah Quincy, Esq., for his Fourth of July Oration delivered at the request of the City of Boston.

"We hail its prophecy and proofs of '*the coming peace*' and his declaration that '*the abolition of war stands forth preëminently as the greatest reform measure that man is now called upon to undertake,*' as worthy of the occasion, and the era in which we live.

"Since Charles Sumner's Oration on 'The True Grandeur of Nations,' delivered July 4, 1845, we know of no address better calculated to advance the cause of Peace to which this Society has been devoted for sixty-three years, and we hereby respectfully request Mr. Quincy to furnish this Society with a copy of it for publication, and as wide circulation as we can give it."

Very respectfully,

ROWLAND B. HOWARD,

Secretary.

BOSTON, MASS., July 22, 1891.

REV. ROWLAND B. HOWARD, *Sec'y American Peace Society:* —

DEAR SIR, — I beg to acknowledge the receipt of your letter of July 13, enclosing a copy of the Resolutions adopted by the American Peace Society. I appreciate very highly the action of the Society, and I am glad to send you herewith a copy of the Oration for publication by it.

Yours very truly,

JOSIAH QUINCY.

THE COMING PEACE.

Mr. Mayor and Fellow-citizens : —

For the one hundred and eighth time the municipality of Boston to-day invites her citizens to join in celebrating the greatest political anniversary that recurs in the calendar of time. Ever since the Fourth of July 1783, when the independence of the United States, declared seven years before, had at last been acknowledged by Great Britain, the day when this nation took its place among the powers of the earth has been commemorated in this city by an unbroken line of municipal orators. The elaborate and scholarly oration of the past, full of classical, literary, and historical allusion, has almost passed away, and is no longer expected; yet it is with diffidence that I enter the excellent fellowship of those who have preceded me in this office, and attempt to add anything to the thoughts which this occasion has suggested.

The recurrence of a national anniversary reminds us that the works of men are not fixed and permanent, but constantly growing and changing. Nations and cities have their birth, their youth, and their maturity. As the child is transformed in growing into the man, so the community is often so changed by the lapse of time that it seems to lose its very identity. The Boston which heard Dr. John Warren deliver her first Fourth of July oration in 1783 has disappeared, and left scarcely a trace behind. The ground upon which she stood, and the harbor in which her ships rode, still remain; yet even these are so altered by the hand of man that our predecessors of a century ago would scarcely recognize them. Of that former Boston little is left but the Old South Church and King's Chapel, the Old State House, the ancient burial grounds, and the Common. Great indeed are the changes which the town and city has seen since this municipal observance was instituted. Her inhabitants have increased from some ten thousand to four hundred and fifty thousand. A population almost wholly native by immediate descent, as well as by birth, has been replaced by a population of which one-third is of foreign birth and two-thirds are of foreign parentage; and to-day one-half of the people of that town which George III. found so rebellious come of ancestors who were loyal subjects of the British throne long after the close of the revolution. In religion, Boston has seen the Church of Rome increasing in the home of Puritanism until nearly one-half of her population is included within its fold. Manufactures have replaced commerce as the leading occupation of her citizens. Fort Hill has been torn down, and the Back Bay has been filled up to be the site of her finest residences. The railroad and the street railway, operated by forces which the last century scarcely knew, daily bring their tens of thousands to swell her trade.

If Boston has changed, the great world beyond her limits has changed no less. In 1783 that world scarcely knew what representative and responsible government meant; it did not know at all what popular government meant on any large scale. Venice and Genoa alone called themselves republics; the Swiss Confederation, the German free cities, the United Provinces of the Netherlands, and Great Britain lived under institutions of some freedom; but elsewhere absolute monarchy or autocracy ruled. Louis XVI. sat

upon the throne of France, which he was to
leave ten years later for the scaffold. Frederick
the Great was still in the last years of his
reign in Prussia. Charles III. was King of
Spain. Catherine the Great was Empress of
Russia. To-day out of the principal independent
nations of the globe, forty-four in number,
twenty-three are republics, and six of these —
Mexico, Brazil, the Argentine Republic, Colum-
bia, Venezuela, and Switzerland — are federal
republics after the type of the United States.
Even of the twenty-one countries having a
monarchical or imperial form of government,
fourteen enjoy representative parliamentary institutions, over which the nominal monarch has only
a partial control. Thus only seven autocratic
governments of any importance now remain in the
world, those of Russia, China, Turkey, Persia,
Siam, Morocco, and Madagascar.

In 1783 there was scarcely a written consti-
tution in existence. To-day, following the example of the United States, all of the republics,
and all of the limited monarchies except Great
Britain and Sweden, have formal, written con-
stitutions, which secure the liberties of the people
and limit the power of their rulers. In form, at

least, the whole American continent, with the
exception of Canada, Newfoundland, the West
India colonies, and a few others of small importance, is now under republican government; and
even Canada, although nominally presided over
by the representative of the British crown, is for
all internal purposes practically governed by her
own people, through parliamentary institutions, as
completely as the United States.

The peculiar significance of this anniversary
lies, therefore, in the fact that the event which
it recalls marks an epoch in the history and in the
political development of mankind. The Declaration of Independence was regarded in 1776 and
long afterward from a purely national point of
view; the Fourth of July appealed to the patriotism of the American rather than to the larger
interests of the citizen of the world. But look-
ing back to-day upon the mighty and beneficent
influence which the political ideas first put into
practice by our forefathers have had upon the
earth, — upon the new aspect which they have
given to civilization, upon the new relations
which they have established and are still establishing between nations, — we feel that we are
carried beyond that narrow and selfish patriotism,

that exclusive regard for the interests of one people, which has too often proved a curse, instead of a blessing, to the world. We are raised to that higher and nobler view which recognizes not only that all men of one nation are free and equal and are joined together as members of a community, but that all peoples and all nations form one great brotherhood of man, and are linked together in one human destiny. As the individual becomes useful and honored by living for his fellow-men, and developing his powers only that he may be capable of rendering his brother better service, so a nation wins respect, not by shutting itself up in a selfish isolation from the world, but by so developing its capacities and resources that they may contribute to the general progress of civilization and the elevation of all mankind.

The most obvious way in which the United States has already rendered a great service to the other peoples of the earth has been in opening its doors to receive them among its citizens and offering its territory for their settlement. While there have been in the remote past, under different conditions of life, great migrations of whole tribes or nations which might compare in magnitude with the movement of population to this country, never in history has there been such a steady flow of immigration as the United States has received since 1820. Never has a nation contained so large a number of inhabitants of foreign birth or of foreign parentage as does ours to-day. Between 1820 and 1890 over 15,000,000 people, nearly one-quarter of the present population of the country, crossed the Atlantic to make their homes upon this side. In ten years alone, from 1880 to 1890, while 7,000,000 were added to our population by birth, over 5,000,000 were added by immigration; a number that exceeds the whole population of the Kingdom of Holland or of the Dominion of Canada, and equals the population of Ireland, or of Scotland and Wales combined. The Anglo-Saxon and the Celt, the Teuton and the Slav, the Scandinavian and the Latin, have all contributed to swell this stream. Never, probably, has there been a country so broadly cosmopolitan in the origin of its people as is the United States to-day, and never have large numbers of immigrants been so readily assimilated and so thoroughly imbued with the spirit of new institutions. However a change in our circumstances, in the condition of Europe, and especially in the character of immigration, may make restrictions upon this free flow of population desirable for the future, nothing can take from us the composite character of our citizenship, or the glory of having furnished new homes to so many millions of our fellow-men, under better and freer conditions than the old world could offer.

With this much by way of introduction, let me come to the special subject upon which I shall address you to-day; a subject as old as man himself, yet still first in importance among the problems which command the attention of the statesman and the philanthropist and affect the welfare of humanity.

The first of these Fourth of July orations was spoken a few months after the signing of the preliminary treaty of peace between the United States and Great Britain. The orator of that day, who had served as a surgeon with the revolutionary forces and knew what war was, spoke with deep feeling of the losses and the suffering which the long conflict had involved, and hailed the return of peace as a supreme blessing. Sixty-two years later, in 1845, Charles Sumner delivered on this same occasion his ora-

tion on " The True Grandeur of Nations," the
best known of any of our Boston Fourth of
July addresses, which, by its masterly condem-
nation of war and unflinching analysis of its
true character, won for its author a high place
among advanced political thinkers. Reflecting
upon the present aspect of the question which
he treated and upon the new light which
the history of the last half century has thrown
upon it, I have felt that no theme would
be more worthy of this anniversary, more in
harmony with the great thoughts which it recalls, or more full of vital import for the present
and the future, than that of The Coming Peace.
Let me attempt, therefore, within the limits imposed upon me, to point out some of the great
forces which are now working on the side of
permanent peace and bringing its attainment within
the range of vision of the statesman and the
philosopher, and to show the connection of this
subject with the past history and present tendencies
of our own country. If in doing this I dwell
chiefly upon considerations connected with the physical welfare and progress of mankind, let it not be
understood that increase of wealth and comfort is
held up as the only worthy object of national

endeavor. A purely material civilization, built upon selfishness instead of brotherhood, destitute of all high ideas and spiritual aims, carries within itself the seeds of its own inevitable decay or downfall. But it is not such a civilization that we need expect as the result of peace.

In this age of reforms the abolition of war — and I include under that term the condition of armed peace which is so peculiarly a feature of our time — stands forth preëminently as the greatest reform measure that man is now called upon to undertake. Others are partial: this is universal. Others may succeed in accomplishing some good: this is sure to bring widespread blessings. Others may improve society or government: this will give the only true basis for society or government to rest upon. Concerning other measures for the amelioration of the world, men may honestly differ; but no one can dispute the beneficence of this, or set a limit upon its good effects. Political economy and religion, science and ethics, the philosophy of politics and the philosophy of history, alike declare the vast mischief that man has suffered, and is still suffering, from war. It degrades the condition of labor and prevents the natural growth of capital; it perverts the moral nature of man; it prevents the evolution of a true civilization; it is the great buttress of autocratic rule and the chief obstruction in the path of popular government. Its crushing burden, while heavier upon some nations, weighs down all. The relief that assured peace would bring would be felt in the remotest corners of the earth, and imagination can scarcely picture the benefits which would follow in its train.

The change in the character of warfare is the first subject that demands our attention as a consideration against its continuance. In no field of human endeavor have methods been more completely revolutionized in the present century by the progress of invention. The men of the revolution would be almost as much at a loss to understand modern methods of fighting as the Indians were to comprehend those of our ancestors. The breech-loading and repeating rifle, the machine gun, the long-range cannon, the armor-plated vessel, the hundred-ton gun, the submarine torpedo, all would be new and strange to them. The quick transportation of troops by steam on land and sea and the military use of the telegraph have alone been sufficient to reverse completely old conditions of conflict. What is to be the effect of these modern methods — just beginning to approach their full development, only

partially tried on land in one great conflict, and that
twenty years ago — upon the future of warfare?

In the first place, recent discoveries have made
quite clear what has long seemed probable, that in
the contest between the forces of destruction and
the means of defence, the ultimate victory must rest
with the former. Man's power to destroy by means
of the high explosives of which so many are now
known, explosives in comparison with which the
action of gunpowder becomes almost insignificant,
must far outrun his power to contrive adequate
defences. The problem of destruction is now a
very simple one in itself, however great may be
the field for the exercise of ingenuity in its solution;
it consists merely in directing explosives to the
point of attack. Let a properly charged torpedo
strike the heaviest armored vessel that can be put
afloat, and she sinks to the bottom of the sea; let
a sufficient charge of dynamite reach any fort that
can be built above ground, and it is shattered and
dismantled. Science and invention have progressed
far enough to make it probable that man will in
the future be able to navigate the air much as he
now navigates the water, and that he will explore
the depths of the ocean as he now skims its surface. Against the submarine torpedo boat capable

of carrying a crew to direct its movements, against the air-ship dropping explosives from the skies, no means of defence will avail. When the arts of destruction have won their final victory, the wars which call them into activity must of necessity cease.

This brings us to another influence which tends towards peace: the enormous cost of modern war and preparations for war, and the immense scale upon which they must be conducted. The best estimates and information show that the six great powers of Europe, namely, Great Britain, France, Germany, Italy, Austria, and Russia, have nearly 3,000,000 men in actual service in time of peace in their armies and navies, while the rest of Europe has 1,000,000 more. The number of fully trained men in the reserves of these great powers is fully equal to twice the number in their standing armies, or 6,000,000 in all, while the number of more or less trained men in Europe, enrolled in the military service and liable to be called out in case of war, amounts to at least 10,000,000, in addition to those counted in the standing armies. It is safe to say that never in the recorded history of the human race have such large numbers of men been under arms in time of peace, or so

many been ready to be called into active service,
as is the case in Europe to-day; and the destruc-
tive power of these armies and navies has never
been approached.   All this means an enormous
financial burden, and makes the waging of war
more a question of finance than it has ever been
before.   The direct money cost of keeping up the
armies and navies of the six great powers of
Europe alone is upward of $600,000,000 a year,
and the indirect cost by the loss of productive
labor must be fully as great; and in order to
measure [properly the cost of war we must add
another sum of at least equal magnitude for the
annual interest upon the war debts of these countries.   The enormous waste of national resources
which these figures feebly express, and the ever-
growing burden which the further development of
the art of war will impose, must inevitably lead to
some readjustment of international relations.   The
expense of the instruments of conflict constantly
increases with their complexity.   No sooner is
one form of rifle perfected than an improved type
supplants it and the old weapon is thrown aside;
with new methods of attack, fortifications and
defences become obsolete and must be replaced by
others at enormous expense; before a ship of war

has been launched more than a few years new vessels are designed and must be built by the nations which are in the struggle for supremacy. All this means a much greater training for the soldier than was formerly requisite; he must be carefully educated in handling his weapons and must understand something of military science. The countries of Europe, groaning beneath the weight of $22,000,000,000 of indebtedness, many of them adding to the burden by constantly recurring deficits, must in the end face one of two alternatives: national bankruptcy and repudiation, or international disarmament.

Even our own recent experience in the United States has shown that the waging of war under a democratic government seems to involve, through the payment of pensions, a new and unforeseen expense of vast proportions, continuing for half a century or more after peace has been reëstablished. Our pension roll to-day amounts to more than the annual cost of the largest army in Europe, and the number of our pensioners is equal to that of the soldiers in any army but that of Russia. Through pensions and interest on war debt we are to-day making an annual payment of over $150,000,000 for a conflict which closed more than

a quarter of a century ago. Expensive as is the
conduct of war under a monarchy, our experience
has shown that its cost is greater yet under a
democracy.

Hostilities under modern conditions are likely to
be as expensive in human life as they are in prop-
erty. On the sea, a ship with a crew of a thousand men may be instantly sunk; on land, if armies
engage each other in open battle, the loss which
modern weapons can inflict will be appalling. A
regiment in line can be mown down by machine
guns like grain beneath the reaper's sickle. Our
civil war cost over half a million lives; with the
progress which warfare has made, the next European war may cost far more.

Another conspicuous agency in promoting peace
is the growing tendency toward popularizing government and placing it upon a basis of responsibility
to the people, if not upon one of pure democracy.
Europe is only just beginning to feel the permanent effects of the American revolution and of the
French revolution. After a century of growth,
republican ideas are stronger than ever before.
The French republic appears at last to be so
firmly established that only some great convulsion
can overthrow it. England has nearly reached

manhood suffrage, and enjoys under the form of a monarchy popular government in the fullest sense, in some respects even outdoing us in democracy; in Germany imperialism has had to take up state socialism in order to retain its hold on the people, and if the pressure of military danger could be removed that country would make rapid strides toward government of the people; even in Italy, Spain, and Portugal the suffrage is widely extended, and republican ideas have a strong foothold. This growth of democracy has an important bearing upon the future of war. In the first place, it removes many of the reasons which have formerly led to conflict. With the diminishing influence of monarchs the causes of enmity arising out of the relations of ruling dynasties are fast being removed, indeed have already largely disappeared. The *casus belli* must now be one which arises out of international, not out of inter-dynastic, relations. Again, the direct and responsible representatives of the people are not likely to go to war unless the people themselves demand it; and making all allowance for national feelings of enmity, affecting whole peoples and races, — such as perhaps still exist between France and Germany, and anciently existed between England and France, —

conflicts between nations are less likely to originate from sentiments shared by all their citizens than from the jealousies or ambitions of a few rulers.

Another influence that makes strongly for peace is the marvellous growth that has taken place in the last half century in the intercourse between nations and the closeness of their relations, arising out of the improvement of means of transportation and communication. These more intimate relations come from increased commerce; from the development of international finance; from the flow of population from one country to another for settlement or travel; from international arrangements in relation to such matters as the postal and telegraph service; and from closer professional, educational, and literary intercourse.

The volume of international commerce, in spite of hostile tariffs, is constantly augmenting at a rapid pace, and, notwithstanding temporary movements in the opposite direction, the thoughtful observer can clearly see that the tendency of the civilized nations is inevitably in the direction of freer trade and the lowering, if not the abolition, of barriers raised for its obstruction. The foreign commerce of England, France, and Germany alone for 1889 was considerably over eight billion dollars.

Already a reaction is seen on the continent against the policy which stands in the way of a yet larger and freer interchange of products. The cable has recently brought us the news of a possible customs union between Germany, Austria, Italy, and Switzerland, and such an event would mean a profound change in the commercial relations of Europe. On our own continent the contest is no longer between the policy of prohibitory duties and freer commerce with all nations, but between the latter policy and special arrangements for reciprocal trade with particular countries.

International financial interests have never approached their present magnitude, and must be powerfully felt in the future in the interest of peace. There are in the first place enormous holdings of national obligations outside of the country issuing them. The bonds of Italy, Spain, Portugal, Russia, Turkey, and other countries are held in very large amounts all over Europe, and are quoted on all the great bourses. The very country that may be urged toward war by political considerations may be held back by financial ones. The fact that Egypt is to-day practically in the hands of a receiver, in order that the interest on her bonds held by foreigners may be paid, is a striking illustration of the power of these international financial interests. The frequent necessity of raising large loans in foreign markets as a preparation for hostilities is also not to be overlooked. Then we must remember that foreign interests in railways and industrial enterprises of various sorts have never been so large as at present. With the decline in the rate of interest which takes place in fully developed countries, capital looks for a better rate of return abroad; it was never so mobile, so easily directed from one country to another, as it is to-day. The modern capitalist has no political or race prejudices; he looks merely to security and profit. The citizens of one country thus become greatly interested in the prosperity and welfare of another; and these are largely dependent on the maintenance of peace.

The extraordinary immigration into this country has already been mentioned; to a lesser degree this transferability of population is noticeable even within the limits of Europe. Modern means of transportation enable labor to flow from one country to another, according to the condition of demand and supply. Every settlement, or even temporary residence, of citizens of one country in another must tend to promote a broad cosmopolitanism and make war less likely. In a less degree travel, upon the enormous scale that it is now conducted, must give the people of the different nations a better knowledge of each other, and so promote, however imperceptibly, a better understanding and more friendly feeling in foreign relations.

The influence of international arrangements for the regulation of such matters of common interest as the postal service, patents, copyrights, coinage, and weights and measures, are considerable factors toward the growth of permanent peace. The Conference of American Republics, recently held at Washington, however small its actual and immediate results may have been, is perhaps the most conspicuous and significant instance ever seen of the friendly meeting of many independent nations to consider subjects of mutual concern. Already, by the action of the governments represented, and at their joint expense, the surveys are being made for an international and an intercontinental railroad to bring them into closer communication. Then there are the great industrial exhibitions, which began only with the last half of this century: surely they are producing effects which cannot be left out of the account.

International organizations of professions or trades, like that of the physicians, which holds its annual meetings successively in different countries; international schools of political thought, like that of socialism; educational institutions, like the great universities of Germany and France, and the schools of painting in Paris and Rome, which draw pupils from all quarters of the earth; the translation and circulation in many countries of all the great works of modern literature; all these influences tend strongly toward bringing about that liberality of spirit and community of thought which is the deadly foe of national hatred. The increase in the knowledge of foreign languages and the growing preponderance of four or five great tongues should also be mentioned; and one of the most characteristic attempts of our time is that of creating a new artificial language, to serve as the common medium of communication of all mankind.

Another general influence which advances peace is the growth of modern industry, and of the facilities for popular education which accompany that growth. While they may exist side by side for a time, industrialism and militarism are in the long run incompatible with each other. Their aims are utterly at variance, the whole spirit of the one is antagonistic to that of the other; the soldier only exists as a parasite upon the operative, and when the latter refuses longer to nourish him, he must either starve or work. The rulers of the past had to govern a people largely rural and agricultural, ignorant and obedient to authority; those of the present have to deal, in the leading, progressive nations, with a population that is largely urban and industrial. The tendency of people to concentrate in cities and large towns is one of the most marked facts that confronts us to-day, and it is full of importance and significance. Industrialism is the cause of modern popular education, because it effects that concentration of population which is a necessary condition of general instruction, and because much of its work demands a certain degree of mental training, hitherto not so necessary for the work required in agriculture. This instruction, slight though it may be, inevitably tends toward the overthrow of the military régime, which has in the past rested mainly upon the ignorance of the people. Above all, the growing popular comprehension of economics, and of the effect and incidence of taxation, must be a powerful factor in checking future wars.

Next in the list of pacific influences is the con-

solidation or unification in a great political aggregate of states formerly independent, the most
striking instances of which in recent times have
been seen in the formation of the Kingdom of Italy
and of the Empire of Germany. It must, indeed,
be conceded that while such a union removes the
danger of warfare between the states which join
together, it seems for the present only to lead to a
greater scale of military preparation for defence
against foreign countries. Yet its tendency in
the end will clearly be a pacific one. An agreement between a few states is much easier to bring
about than one between many. The affairs of nations, like those of industry, can be managed with
less friction when a few men can enter into engage-
ments of wide and far-reaching scope. With the
absolute control of the destinies of Europe lodged
in the hands of a few great powers, a small number of influential statesmen should be able at an
opportune moment to secure its permanent peace.

Among the civilizing movements of the age
which are now making for peace, the growth of the
sentiment of humanity, of international solidarity,
of the brotherhood of man, must be set down
as one of the most important. The forces before
touched upon, though partly connected with the

intellectual life of mankind, have mainly been
related to its material well-being. But this last
influence rests upon the perception of the spiritual
and eternal which underlies the material and the
mental, and transcends both. In no respect has
the growth of the race been more marked during the present century than in the development
of those qualities which are described by the
word humanity. Institutions and organizations of
charity and benevolence, of which this city has
so many, are the growth of the present century.
Even with the development of modern warfare
there have sprung up great voluntary organizations to mitigate its horrors and to lighten its
sufferings, to give aid to those who have been
disabled by its perils and to carry succor to the
widow and the orphan. Side by side with the
heroes of the battlefield we have in modern times
placed the heroines of the hospital. Political and
social philosophies based on universal brotherhood, teaching the doctrines of world-wide democracy and equality and of the true community
of all human interests, are at last reaching the
great body of the people and appealing to their
minds and hearts. More and more is it recognized that under modern conditions the na-

tions of the earth are drawn together and made
one people. The social problem and the labor
problem are international in their scope, and
must be international in their solution; for, however the interests of a class in one nation may
be hostile to the interests of a class in another,
the interests of the masses of the people are
everywhere and always the same. Injustice cannot exist in one country without inflicting harm
on others. By lifting the burdens in one community the life of all mankind is made a little better.
The social readjuster cannot proceed far without
discovering that, if he should succeed in carrying out his plans for improvement in his own
nation, it would be swamped by immigration
from all others; the labor reformer soon learns,
as the imperial young ruler of Germany lately
recognized by calling an international labor conference at Berlin, that any radical steps for
the elevation of the manual workers call for
international action. The industrial organization,
when effected upon that more equitable basis for
which good men are striving, must finally bring
us to that awakening of the race consciousness
which gives the truest perception of the purposes
of life.

In this connection, one fact which tends strongly to the growth of this broad humanity should not be overlooked; I allude to the great change that has taken place in the position of woman. After being kept through the recorded history of the world, with rare exceptions, in the position of the drudge or the plaything of man, without any place of her own in the body social or the body politic, woman to-day finds in the most advanced nations that nearly all professions and occupations are open to her; and if she is not yet accorded the franchise, she is admitted to have an equal interest with man in political questions and an equal right to form her own opinions and to declare them. The influence of woman is to-day a most potent factor in all humanitarian movements, and therefore is indirectly a check upon war; and as her sphere of influence and of action goes on widening, she must be strongly felt as a direct power in favor of the maintenance of peace.

The removal in modern times of many of the causes which formerly led to hostilities is worthy of notice. With the acceptance of the idea of religious toleration, differences of creed no longer furnish the incentive to war which they have so often done in the past.   Interference in the internal affairs of other countries is limited to semi-civilized states, and the doctrine of the Holy Alliance, that war could properly be waged against a country on account of obnoxious changes in its political institutions, has become a curiosity of history.   With the occupation of almost every portion of the earth's surface, the occasion of conflicts for the possession of new territory is removed; and we have lately seen the greater part of the only continent that still remains unsettled by civilized men amicably divided between the nations of Europe.   The change in the relation between colonies and the mother country no longer leaves room for such a war as that of the revolution.   The same nation that imposed vexatious laws upon the American colonies, and would not allow the bond of connection to be severed until hostilities had lasted for seven years, has accorded to Canada and Australia almost absolute powers of self-government, and would not fire a shot to keep either of them in the British empire against the will of its people.   The doctrine of preserving the balance of power in Europe, which in former times was held to justify hostile measures against any state which was acquiring a preponderating strength, has become completely obsolete.

The neutralization of small states by treaty between the great powers is significant as confining the sphere of conflict. Thus Switzerland and Belgium have both been eliminated from possible European struggles, and the neutrality of their territory has been formally guaranteed. By the extension of international law the rights of neutrals and of non-combatants have been largely protected. By the Geneva Convention of 1864 the hospital service was placed under the protection of the Red Cross. Just as the growth of the common law restrained the action of the individual and forced him to regard the interests of others, so the growth of a common law of nations has surrounded their action in war with a constantly growing body of regulations, of which all civilized countries recognize the binding force; and regulated warfare is a long step toward peace.

The actual nature of military conflict and the horrors of battle have never before been brought home to the great body of the people as they have been in our time; and the more generally war is understood the less likely it is to be

tolerated. The modern newspaper lays before
its hundreds of thousands of readers a graphic
account of actual operations in the field; the war
correspondent depicts hardship and suffering, dis-
ease and wounds, the agony of death, as well as
the triumphs of arms; even the art of painting
has been pressed into the same service, and vivid
pictures of great artists have perpetuated the
ghastly scenes of the battlefield.

The conclusion that the world will outgrow
war to which we are thus led by a brief survey
of the forces which are now promoting peace
is supported by some additional considerations
which are worthy of notice. These fall under
the heads of practicable substitutes for war, the
teachings of scientific evolution, and the influence
of religion.

Negotiation and arbitration are the two great
substitutes for war. Modern methods of quick
communication have made lengthy negotiations
possible without unreasonable delay; in these the
points of difference can be gradually narrowed
down and finally settled. Where the intention to
seize a pretext for quarrel exists, of course there
is never any difficulty in making negotiation fail;
but if there is a fair intention on both sides to

reach an understanding, modern diplomacy can generally effect it, or can at least arrive at an agreement for arbitration in those cases which can best be settled in that manner. Such negotiations are now conducted not through ambassadors at a distance, to whose discretion much must be trusted, but through direct communications between the responsible heads of the state departments or foreign offices. The long series of successful instances of arbitration, now more than sixty in number during the present century, go far to prove the possibility of dispensing with the arbitrament of the sword. A most conspicuous example was the Geneva arbitration, conducted between Great Britain and the nation which declared her independence on the day we celebrate; and last year was made memorable by the meeting at Washington of an International Conference of all the republics of America, to whose work I shall again refer.

Experience has shown that international tribunals can be constituted that are as competent and as unprejudiced in the settlement of international controversies as are the courts of law in passing upon disputes between individuals. As the private war and trial by battle have become obsolete, and even duelling is now held in contempt, so it is not unreasonable to indulge the hope that in coming time the arbitrament of war, crude in its working and uncertain in its results, will be replaced by the arbitrament of peace. To-day, in the Supreme Court of the United States, the highest judicial tribunal ever instituted, two States of the Union, possessed of all the attributes of sovereignty save such as they have surrendered to the federal government, appear as parties to a suit and yield obedience to the court's decree. In the future we may well believe that the nations of the earth will establish a yet more exalted tribunal of justice, to which they will be content to submit all controversies, and by whose judgment they will cheerfully abide.

The teachings of scientific evolution lead us to the same conclusion as to the probability of the outgrowing of war. The fruitful conceptions as to the origin, growth, and development of man, of human society, and of political institutions which science has opened to us during the last half century, confirm the faith that the progress of mankind is from barbarism and strife to civilization and brotherhood. The military or-ganization of society was suitable to a stage of development that we are rapidly leaving, and must give place to a purely industrial organization. Evolution teaches us that the present has grown out of a past from which it differs as widely as possible in every conceivable respect, and that many of the qualities in man which were once regarded as a part of his nature are comparatively recent acquisitions. It also teaches us that from the present we cannot judge of the future, that as man has been modified, physically, mentally, and morally, by his past experience on earth, so he will continue to change in the time to come. The brutality of the savage has given place to the humanity of the civilized man; and peace is the goal toward which the latter is tending in his process of evolution. As the race expresses itself through the unit, and is typified in it, so we may well conclude that as man as an individual has, through the long progress of ages, become more and more a pacific animal, only making war in his associated capacity, so the race will in future acquire the same character.

Finally, for those who have any religious belief in the spiritual significance of this earth, the abolition of war must appear as something that

will inevitably come. If this globe has any
higher purpose than to serve as the arena upon
which human gladiators are to fight, then the
period of conflict must one day give place to that
millennium proclaimed by the prophet, when " nation shall not lift sword against nation, neither
shall they learn war any more." In promoting
this growth of religious sentiment against war,
Christianity can win one of its noblest triumphs.
Slowly and gradually the different spheres of
man's activity have been brought more and
more under the sway of the principles of the
Gospel, far as these still are from exerting
their proper influence; and at last its precepts
must be applied to international relations. That
higher and more spiritual Christianity which the
nineteenth century has developed — higher because returning more closely to the point from
which it started in the first century — is by
no means the least of the forces which in our
time strengthen the cause of peace; and surely
it is capable of becoming by far the greatest.
One of the distinctive features of early Christianity
was that it broke down the conventional barriers
between Jew and Gentile, between Roman and
barbarian, and declared that in the divine mind

there were no distinctions of nationality or race. It brought to all humanity the good tidings of universal brotherhood. And though for long centuries men who preached the gospel of peace have given their sanction to war, celebrating its victories and blessing its conquerors, yet the modern revival of a truer understanding of the teachings of Christ, if it does not result in the acceptance of the doctrine of non-resistance so nobly maintained by one body of his followers, must at least lead to the conviction that war is un-Christian and unnecessary.

Thus far I have spoken of the influences that affect warfare between nations. Civil contests within the limits of a single country demand separate mention. Several of the considerations already alluded to apply to internal conflicts; but the great security for the maintenance of domestic peace arises from the fact that some governments have already reached a condition of stable equilibrium under democratic institutions, and that many others are fast tending to that point. While popular government is establishing itself, while it is so far ahead of the political capacity of the masses of the people that they become the prey of demagogues or autocrats, it may indeed seem to occasion more insurrections and civil conflicts than monarchical rule. But this is only a temporary phase which is outgrown. No government that the world has yet devised is as stable as a democracy whose people understand their rights of sovereignty. When every citizen is free to cast a secret ballot, and every political change which a majority desire can be secured by the action of their representatives, all occasion for armed revolution has passed away, and the rebel against the government is a traitor to the people.

And now how shall we connect these thoughts with the anniversary of to-day, and what place shall we assign to our own country in this progress of the world toward peace? In the first place we must remember that, though the Declaration of Independence led to a long and bloody war, it was, on our part, purely a defensive war. Our forefathers were fighting upon their own territory, for the right to govern themselves. Slow and reluctant in entering upon war, prosecuting it under extreme difficulties, they were glad to welcome peace as soon as their independence was acknowledged. The principles which they proclaimed are entirely opposed to wars of aggression. If all

men are created equal, if as individuals they stand
upon an even footing, then also must they be equal
in their associated capacity as nations, and the
poorest and the feeblest nation is equal in all its
rights to the richest and the strongest; then must
the same code of morals apply to governments in
their dealings with each other that applies to men;
then must the ignoble rule upon which the world
has lived so long, that in the affairs of nations
might makes right, give place to the law of justice. In the course of more than a century of
national life, our country has been true in the
main to its pacific character. The pages of our
history are indeed blotted with the record of two
wars with foreign countries; it is true, also, that
our land has been the scene of the greatest civil
conflict that the world has ever known. But now
for nearly eighty years our relations with the
mother country, though subjected to some strain at
times, have remained on a friendly footing, and
many embarrassing questions between us have been
settled by peaceful methods; and the fact that the
slave power once engaged us in war with Mexico
has long since been forgotten on both sides of the
line, in the friendly intercourse of commerce. The
war of the rebellion was fought to secure the con-

ditions of lasting peace by maintaining the integrity of the federal union. The United States as one nation has a pacific mission to fulfil on earth, and the war that established once for all that the federal government is an indissoluble union of indestructible States, as it was fought by peaceful citizens, so it had peace for its end and object. The blood of the brave men of the North and of the South, mingling upon the battlefield, has but more firmly cemented the union of two sections in a common country.

Our nation has rendered a great service to the cause we are considering by setting an example against the practice of maintaining a large standing army. Never, in modern history at least, has any great nation kept so small a proportion of its citizens under arms as has the United States. To-day, with a population of 63,000,000 and a territory of over 3,500,000 square miles, our standing army still remains within the limit of 25,000 men, established many years ago, so that we have only one soldier for every twenty-five hundred people. Our army numbers but little more than a national police force; probably the combined policemen of a score of our largest cities would equal numerically all the troops of the Union. And when, at the close of the civil war, a million men who had been drawn from civil pursuits and transformed for the time being into soldiers, returned again, easily and quietly, to the ordinary affairs of life, another great lesson was taught to mankind. To-day not alone the geographical separation of our country from others renders it secure, but the paradox must be acknowledged that its very devotion to peaceful industry makes it so strong in the resources required for modern warfare that we need not fear the attack of any foreign power. There is not a nation that now groans beneath the burden of a great standing army that would not be stronger as a warlike power at the end of ten years if it could follow our example and devote itself to industrial development during that time.

But perhaps the most important service which we have rendered to the establishment of peace lies in our development of the federal system of government. Here has been successfully solved the political problem which has been the puzzle of past ages. The great empires of the past involved so much centralization of power that they broke down of their own weight. Not until our forefathers conceived and put into practice the idea of a federal nation of limited powers, made up of states which chose their own executive officers and legislative bodies, and which retained all the powers of sovereignty except such as they conferred upon the central government by a formal, written instrument, did any practicable way appear of combining great numbers of men permanently under one political organization. In our system we have laid down the lines of future political development, and have furnished the model upon which not only three of the republics of America, but the empires of Germany and of Austria-Hungary, the Dominion of Canada, and the new Commonwealth of Australia, have already been formed. The world now knows how it is possible, under free institutions, to form a closer political union and a more coherent empire than autocratic rule has ever been able to create, and along this path of political progress lies the road to the permanent abolition of war.

The United States has always contributed powerfully to hasten the coming disarmament by its encouragement of arbitration as a means of settling international disputes, and by the support which its people have given to the conception of a Congress of Nations as the final consummation to be aimed at. The very idea of an international tribu-

nal seems to have originated two centuries ago
with one of the founders of America, who has
given his name to one of our greatest common-
wealths. In 1693 William Penn, in an "Essay on
the Present and Future Peace of Europe," urged
the plan of a general congress for the settlement
of international disputes. The first organized
movement in support of this idea began with the
formation of the American Peace Society in 1828;
its founders declared that they hoped "to increase and promote the practice already begun of
submitting national differences to amicable discus-
sion and arbitration, and finally of settling all
national controversies by an appeal to reason, as
becomes rational creatures, and not by physical
force, as is worthy only of brute beasts; and this
shall be done," they continued, "by a congress of
Christian nations, whose decrees shall be enforced
by public opinion." As long ago as 1835 the Legis-
lature of this Commonwealth passed resolutions
declaring that some mode should be established
for the amicable and final adjustment of all international disputes, instead of resorting to arms.

By the treaty of Washington, submitting its just
claim against Great Britain to arbitration, our
country in a conspicuous instance showed her

opposition to unnecessary war. But perhaps her greatest service to this means of settlement will come from an attempt which has unhappily proved abortive for the present. By the treaty agreed to by the representatives of the American republics, assembled in International Conference at Washington at the invitation of the United States, it is declared that "believing that war is the most cruel, the most fruitless, and the most dangerous expedient for the settlement of international differences, the republics of America hereby adopt arbitration as a principle of American international law for the settlement of the differences, disputes, or controversies that may arise between two or more of them." Arbitration is by this treaty made obligatory in every case except where one of the parties to the controversy believes that the point at issue is of such a nature as to threaten its national independence; and this exception simply corresponds to the right to resort to force in defence of his life which the law everywhere allows to the individual man. A code of rules for putting arbitration into practice is embodied in the treaty, and it is provided that any other nation may become a party to it. The unfortunate failure of the nations represented to ratify this treaty within the time allowed has for the present prevented the accomplishment of its beneficent purposes; yet even its adoption by the Conference marked an epoch in international relations. This body took further steps of importance in recommending the respective governments to adopt the declaration that "the principle of conquest shall not be recognized as admissible under American public law," and in declaring its desire that European nations, by becoming parties to the treaty, should adopt its methods of settling disputes between themselves and the nations of America.

And now, with this record in the past, what can we still do in the future to promote that union of different races which has taken place to so wonderful an extent upon our own territory; how can we help further to perfect that brotherhood of man upon which our political institutions are founded? First of all, we can continue to hold before the eyes of the world the spectacle of a peaceful, federal republic, already exceeding in its population every government in the world except the empires of China, Russia, and Great Britain, and exceeding even the latter if the two hundred and fifty millions of her subjects in India are omitted. We stand to-day among the four great powers of the earth, surpassed by none in the extent of our resources, equalled by none in the intelligence of our people. It must be that the United States will have more and more power in moulding the public opinion of the world, and that our example and practice will have a growing influence upon other nations. Therefore every effort to elevate and purify American political or social life, to keep the stream of democracy flowing clear and unobstructed, to make government of the people work more successfully, is also an effort to promote the concord of nations and to hasten the coming peace.

But the time has now arrived when the United States can do more to promote this cause than merely securing her own internal development. With the final settlement of the once menacing questions of slavery and secession, with the final establishment of the national government on a firm foundation, we can turn our attention to our relations with other countries. We can in the future play a continually increasing part in that growing closeness of intercourse between nations which has already been referred to as one of the strongest promoters of peace. In the way of commerce, having already established within our borders complete freedom of trade on the largest scale which the world has ever seen, we shall in the future seek, as we are already doing, closer trade relations with foreign countries; and every barrier to commerce that is removed, whether by treaty of reciprocity or otherwise, raises another barrier against war. The imaginary lines that separate our country from Canada on the north and Mexico on the south must, in respect to commerce at least, fade away before the true community of interest which unites us with them. With the rapid strides which we are making in the higher forms of civilization, the friendly ties of common intellectual and professional interests must bring us into closer association with European countries; the establishment this year of the long-delayed right of international copyright has been one step toward the connection of nations through literature. Even the American inventors who are furnishing improved weapons of warfare to foreign countries may be, as we have seen, hastening the extinction of war and coöperating in the true mission of their nation.

We live in an age of searching analysis, when the oldest and most cherished institutions are obliged to submit to a critical examination and dissection. When the people are sufficiently educated in all countries, as they are fast becoming in some, to understand the true nature of war, they will insist upon its abolition. Already, in almost every country of Europe except England, the maintenance of the standing army rests not upon free will, but upon force; the ranks are not filled up by the volunteer, but by the conscript. The people, if left to themselves, would engage in the pursuits of civil life; hence the necessity for universal compulsory service in order to keep up militarism. In England, with her much smaller army, it is true that its numbers are, with some difficulty, maintained by voluntary enlistment; but her experience furnishes a scarcely less striking commentary on the dislike of the people for military service. Recruits have to be drawn mainly from the dregs of the population; and at the expiration of their term of service more than nine men out of ten refuse all inducements to reënlist. Within the last ten years there have been over forty thousand deserters. The plain truth is that, unless driven by necessity, men will not serve in standing armies in time of peace; and in time of war, unless some great cause appeals to their convictions, as it did to the soldiers of the revolution, modern citizens must have their passions roused and their emotions excited before they will fight. Leave out the music, the banners, and the uniforms, the pride, pomp, and circumstance which give to war its fictitious glory, and it would be a sorry game, at which few would care to play. Far be it from me to depreciate the heroic self-sacrifice which men have shown in responding to what they believed to be their country's call to honorable duty; but it cannot be denied that if the peoples of the past had been as free and as intelligent as our people are to-day, they would have fought very few of the wars which have stained the pages of history. As liberty and education advance hand in hand, as the citizen assumes control over his own actions and learns to use his own reason, as he comes to discern the real essence and substance of war underneath its external forms and trappings, he will refuse longer to lend himself to the destruction of human life.

Let it not be thought that the considerations that have been brought forward are meant to lead to the conclusion that there will be no more war in the world, and that the great armies of Europe will

be peacefully reduced and finally disbanded. This
may indeed come to pass, however unlikely it may
seem; yet, if the probabilities of the immediate
present only were considered, the topic of this address might more appropriately be The Coming
War. Before the sword can be finally sheathed
it may be that the soil of Europe is to be again
drenched in blood. The darkest hour in the history
of war may be yet to come; but it will be a dark-
ness that presages dawn. No one of the influences
that have been touched upon may yet be strong
enough to stifle the voices that cry to arms; but in
the aggregate, and in the fulness of time, their silent
effect will be irresistible. We cannot fix a date
for the cessation of war, and it will hardly come
in what remains of the nineteenth century; yet it
may come in the twentieth, and some within the
sound of my voice may live to look back upon it
as an outgrown barbarism, as to-day we look back
upon the quarrels of the feudal barons, upon trial
by battle, and upon duelling. It has been well said
that many disappointments and misunderstandings
arise from the fact that man is in a hurry and the
Creator is not. "The kingdom of God cometh
not with observation;" the arrival of peace draws
near slowly and imperceptibly, but none the less

surely. To our brief span of mortality the period of strife that yet remains might, if we knew its duration, seem long; but to Him in whose sight a thousand years are but as yesterday it is as nothing. Compared with the ages through which the hand of man has been against his fellow-man, and nation has met nation in mortal battle, such survival of conflict as may yet remain will be of insignificant duration. "It is really a thought," says Emerson, "that built this portentous war establishment, and a thought shall also melt it away." The anniversary that we celebrate to-day can serve no nobler purpose than to promote this higher thought. The memory of the founders of the republic cannot be more highly honored than by recognizing the federation of all races as the true outcome of their work. The religion of Christ cannot be better exemplified than in hastening the coming of "peace on earth, good will to men."